THE HERESY
OF
POPULAR
SOVEREIGNTY

The Heresy of Popular Sovereignty

Fr. Charles Maignen

Translated from the French

La souveraineté du peuple est une hérésie

Stabat Mater Press

This work, *La souveraineté du peuple est une hérésie* (1892), by Fr. Charles Maignen, has been translated and republished by Stabat Mater Press.
The original work was written and published in French and is in the public domain. This English edition is copyright © 2025 – Stabat Mater Press.

No part of this book may be reproduced, stored in a retrieval system, or transmitted in any form or by any means—electronic, mechanical, photocopying, recording, or otherwise—without the prior written permission of the publisher, except in the case of brief quotations used in reviews, scholarly articles, or other critical works.

Published by Stabat Mater Press
www.stabatmaterpress.com

Cover design and interior typesetting by Stabat Mater Press. All artwork not cited is in the public domain.
Printed in the United States of America

ISBN (Paperback): 979-8-9997560-5-3

*"For he must reign until he has put all
his enemies under his feet"*

1 Corinthians 15:25

Contents

Editor's Preface   1

Introduction   5

Part I
GOD AND POWER

    1. The Origin of Society and Civil Power   13

    2. Nature and Purpose of Civil Society   21

    3. Civil Power   27

    4. The Best Form of Government   43

PART II
REVOLUTIONARY DOCTRINE

    5. The Principles   53

    6. Sovereignty of Man   57

    7. Liberty   63

8. Equality	67
9. Revolutionary Form of Government	71

PART III
REASON AND FAITH

10. Judgement of Theologians	79
11. Doctrines of the Holy See	87

PART IV
CONCLUSION

12. Theorical Conclusions	99
13. Practical Conclusions	107
14. The Obstacle	111
NOTES	115

Editor's Preface

This little book comes thundering like King Henry's own charge on St. Crispin's Day. The blunt Father Maignen announces what every Catholic peasant once knew, and every modern now denies: that power comes from Almighty God, that society stands or rots accordingly regarding that truth, and that the modern substitute — this unintelligibility about the People as a kind of gaseous deity — is rank heresy. This fact will make the comfortable modern wince. Let him wince! Heresy it is, and Father Maignen names it so with the old French precision that built Chartres and Sainte-Chapelle.

His argument is clear: Civil life arises from nature as Almighty God created it; families join into a polity; authority emerges as the soul of this corporate body; the soul receives life from Almighty God. Father Maignen plants his standard with the help of Aquinas, Suarez, and centuries of Catholic Political Thought. He grants their careful distinctions and keeps the doctrine clean without the sentimental fog so apparent in modern political philosophy.

He then proceeds to the present malady. Popular sovereignty claims a throne which rightly belongs to Christ the King. Once a people treats its own collective will as first principle, the state claims to invent rights and abolish duties, and the Church receives "toleration" as a favor from a creature. That arrangement breeds the two twins of our century: libertinism in morals and managerial, bureaucratic despotism in practice.

The modern reader meets this book in a season of managed crises. The media-machine manufactures emergency; the false dichotomy of the political party-machine manufactures consent; the court-machine manufactures new, false rights that trump the Natural Law. Each machine serves a theology, even when it swears that it serves none. Maignen rightly unmasks the theology: man enthroned, Almighty God relegated to the private corner, Christ the King reduced to a poorly-used political slogan, or a decorative emblem on civic holidays. A society cannot thrive under this not-so-polite blasphemy.

The editor prays that the reader will find the undoubtable, seasoned truths in this work. The Enlightenment project has failed, and it is well past due to treat Christ as King once more. Our current political arrangement that treats the people as a mystical source of being sets itself against the Creator's act.

Father Maignen exhorts Catholics to engage in politics to educate conscience, to proclaim the Kingship of Christ, and to insist that rulers face the law of Almighty God as something real. The saint in the voting booth and the magistrate at his desk are forced to ask themselves the same question: who gives the right to command? The Catholic should know the answer. Sermons, schools, guilds, families, confraternities, and newspapers once carried this answer through a civilization. They can carry it again.

For the first time since its original publication in 1892, this work has been reproduced in English for the modern reader. This edition serves the concrete aim to reclaim the Social Kingship of Our Lord Jesus Christ in our overburdened world. There may be a litany of works of political philosophy that abstractly treat "governance," yet the simple Catholic father, the humble parish priest, or the university student need a brief and lucid book that sets forth the Social Kingship of Christ.

A brief word, as well, for those who fear *integralism* as a bogeyman. Father Maignen proposes integration in the classical sense: an order where temporal power pursues the common good within its own sphere and acknowledges the spiritual end of man as the higher measure. This arrangement requires virtue, craft, and prudence; it also brings peace. History offers proof. Where rulers honored the law of God, families grew, courts rendered judgment without cynicism, and artisans built cities that taught children to look up.

A final exhortation. Read the introduction as a manifesto and the subsequent chapters as a course of treatment. Carry the distinctions into parish study circles, college reading groups, and editorial rooms. Measure current proposals by the principles set out here: origin of society, nature of authority, end of the state, limits of the state, supremacy of the moral law, rights and immunities of the Church, dignity of the family, hierarchy of associations within the body politic, and the social reign of Christ the King as the crown of all. These principles possess the strength of reality. They will outlast polling cycles and professional outrage.

May our Lord Jesus Christ, true King and Lawgiver, receive public honor from a people that remembers where authority begins and where freedom finds its form.

All Saint's Day, 2025
Editor, Stabat Mater Press

Introduction

What divides France into two camps is not the form of government, but the principle of authority.

We are faced with two doctrines: that of the Church: "All power comes from God", and that of the Revolution: "All power comes from the people."

Both can be adapted to different forms of political power. The first found its application in the republics of Venice, Genoa, and the Swiss cantons, as well as in the French monarchy. The second dominated constitutional monarchies, such as the three republics that have succeeded one another in France since the Revolution.

Therefore, not everything is said when one proclaims oneself a republican or a monarchist; it would be better to say whether one is a supporter or an opponent of the sovereignty of the people.

Why, in practice, does the division manifest itself more in the form than in the principle of authority? Is it pure ambiguity and misunderstanding? No. It is because, in reality, while all political forms are compatible with both doctrines, there are nevertheless some that correspond more fully to one or the other.

Philosophy teaches that monarchy is the best form of government, and if the Church were ever to pronounce on the question of principle, without proscribing any regular form, it would do so in this sense.

We know, on the other hand, that the supporters of popular sovereignty prefer the republic to the monarchy, even a constitutional one, and establish it or tend to establish it everywhere.

It is therefore natural that in France, a country of logic and extreme consequences, the struggle between the two principles is manifested by the struggle between the political forms which are, each in its own way, the most perfect expression of them.

First of all, we must clearly pose the question, as it stirs in people's minds, in order to have a touchstone that allows the true children of the Church to recognize each other, and that creates unity by separating the wheat from the chaff.

If Catholics are divided, it is because they are not sufficiently separated from their enemies. Many are taken in by appearances and formulas; the fundamental subject of the debate must be brought to light and highlighted, and the enemy must be shown where he lies, if we truly want to defeat him.

The revolutionary dogma of popular sovereignty; that is the enemy!

As long as this error dominates minds, there will not be a single government in the world that can remain Christian.

A Christian monarchy will be impossible, for want of a people who know how to obey and a king who dares to command. A Christian republic will be even more impossible, because it is senseless to establish a popular government where the people recognize no limits to their sovereignty. Therefore, all the efforts of the Church and Catholics must be directed toward this goal: to proclaim the downfall of man who has usurped God's place in society!

The Church will do it one day.

It will condemn the fundamental dogma of the Revolution:

"If anyone says that sovereignty does not come from God, but from the people and resides essentially in the nation, let him be anathema."

This will be a day of triumph!

But, in the meantime, we Catholics speak out, and proclaim loudly, in the face of the revolutionary beast, drunk on the blood of the souls it devours, the social kingship of Our Lord Jesus Christ, the unique source and sole master of all sovereignty.

This, I admit, is a program that would not be well received by voters, and this is the problem that has made the programs written so far by Catholics insufficient and ineffective.

But the Catholic party's program must not be an electoral program.

The Church cannot establish the people as the judge of their disputes with the State.

If we subject His rights and immunities to the verdict of the sovereign people, we are indeed guilty.

Let us take part in political struggles to educate, not to seduce.

Let us teach the people that if they want good rulers, they must consent to having masters.

Let us remind him that He holds, against common sense and justice, the inalienable rights of sovereign power, and, if we descend into the political arena, let it not be to say to Him the Hail Caesar of the gladiators, but the Credo of the martyrs.

Our first task in this work will be to study Catholic doctrine on the nature, origin, and end of society, as well as on the origin and best form of social power and government. We will then examine the essential principles of revolutionary doctrine and the political institutions most suited to the application of these doctrines.

In the light of Catholic teaching, we will critique the political regime of the Revolution, and we will show what it contains that is incompatible with the doctrine and the very existence of the Church.

Finally, we will endeavor to draw some conclusions from this work: theoretical conclusions for doctrine, practical conclusions for action.

Part I
GOD AND POWER

Chapter One

The Origin of Society and Civil Power

What is the origin of civil society? Before answering this question, it is necessary to clearly define its meaning, because the origin of society can be considered from the point of view of history or from the point of view of doctrine.

It is to Christian philosophy that we will first turn to answer us and tell us why it is necessary for man to live in society.

Man, says Saint Thomas Aquinas, cannot be self-sufficient.[1]

How could an isolated individual obtain everything necessary for their food? How would they prepare clothing, remedies, and shelter? How would they simultaneously make their tools for work?

Remaining alone, he could not make sufficient use of his time and strength to devote to study, manual labor, and the care of his food what is necessary, however, for a man to reach the full development of his physical strength and moral faculties.

It is true that 18th-century philosophers claimed that this state of ignorance and isolation was the natural state of man; but, in a singular contradiction, they admitted that if humanity had not emerged from this state of nature to form societies, it would have inevitably perished.

A singular state of nature, certainly, which would have led human nature to its destruction! This admission alone can suffice to prove the truth of the Catholic thesis: for the natural state of a creature must be favorable to its preservation and to the perfection of its faculties.

Now, this state, which favors the preservation and improvement of the human species, is the social state. The true state of nature is therefore that of man living in society with his fellow human beings.

But there are several kinds of society among men. The first, the most natural, the most necessary of all, is the family, which provides man with the first and most indispensable means of preserving and maintaining life. It is the family that, through marriage, ensures the multiplication of humankind on earth; it is the family that provides children with the varied care required by the delicacy of their bodies and the ignorance of their minds; it is the family that bestows pure and faithful affections.

But it is not the only necessary society. What we have said of the isolated individual can, in proportion, be applied to the family, if it does not find in a larger and stronger society the complement it needs.

It too cannot be entirely self-sufficient. Will it be able, by its own resources alone, to engage in the diverse industries required for a reasonable degree of comfort and well-being in clothing, food, and housing? Will its members be able, on their own, to acquire the extensive and demanding knowledge necessary for the proper practice of these various industries? Will they be able to devote themselves to the study of the sciences, insofar as they are necessary for the normal development of the intellect? Finally, will they be able to resist their enemies and take justice into their own hands without infringing upon the rights of others?

An isolated family, placed outside of any society, and having nothing that it does not have to draw from its own resources, will necessarily be in great poverty of the goods that man needs for the development of his faculties.

Thus, families are compelled by necessity to unite in a more perfect society, just as individuals are driven by an even more compelling need to gather around a hearth. This society, called upon to compensate for the inadequacy of domestic society and to ensure, at the same time, its preservation and prosperity within the framework of public order, is commonly referred to by authors as civil society or political society. Its origin, its raison d'être, lies in natural law itself, that is to say, God, who is its rule and its author.

It is God who created man in such a way that he cannot live without the institution of the family; therefore, it is God who is the author of the family. It is God, the author of the family, who made this initial society insufficient in itself, so that families have a natural tendency to unite and form civil society; therefore, God is the author of civil society.

Thus, the primary cause of civil society is God; its proximate cause is the nature of man, its immediate cause is the nature of the family.

This, in a few words, is the answer of Catholic philosophy to our question: What is the origin of civil society?[2]

Let us now examine history. This is not about going back to the origin of each civil society, of each nation, but only to the origin of the first society, the one before which there were only families.

The entire history of the origins of our race is contained in the first chapters of Genesis; the facts it relates are attested by the very authority of God:

therefore, there are none that can present a greater character of certainty.

In these facts, we find striking confirmation of the doctrine formulated above. In the beginning, God creates a single man, but he soon adds: "It is not good for man to be alone."[3] He gives him a companion, "adjutorium simile sibi," and the family is founded.[4]

Man sinned before the family could give birth to another society; should we conclude that civil society would not have existed if Adam had persisted in a state of innocence?

It would be too hasty to resolve a question on which great theologians have opposing opinions and which, moreover, is irrelevant.

In any case, it is a fact that civil society, presupposing the plurality of families, could not have formed, and indeed did form, until after a certain spread of humankind across the earth. However, the formation of society was contemporaneous with the first humans. Genesis makes the first mention of the founding of a city, after the murder of Abel by his brother.[5]

Cain was not the only son of Adam to give birth to a city, and, before the end of his long career, the father of all men was able to see numerous and flourishing cities spring up from this land that God had given him to be made fruitful by his labor.

The primary factor that determined the formation of ancient political societies was the expansion and multiplication of families from the same stock, remaining united at first by purely domestic ties, then, little by little, by relations of a public and legal nature.

Subsequently, conquest, treaties, or the free consent of many served as the starting point for the formation of numerous states; but the original community remains the natural fact that gives birth to cities. This is what Cicero expressed thus: "Prima societas in ipso conjugio est, proxima in liberis, deinde una domus, communia omnia. Id autem est principium urbis et quasi seminarium reipublicae." (De Officiis).

Thus, philosophy and history agree that society is willed and required by nature, and that the theories of the Social Contract are no less contradictory to facts than to reason. In the encyclical "Immortale Dei," the Sovereign Pontiff summarized Catholic doctrine: "Man," he said, "is born to live in society, for in isolation he cannot procure what is useful and necessary for life, nor acquire perfection of mind and heart; Providence has made him to unite with his fellow men in a society, both domestic and civil, the only one capable of providing what is necessary for the perfection of existence." Already, in the Encyclical "Diuturnum illud", the Pope had said even more briefly and with more force: "Magnus est error non videre, id quod manifestum est, homines, quum non sint solivagum genus, citra liberam ipsorum voluntatem ad naturalem communitatem esse natos"; and, speaking of the Social Contract, he added: "Ac proeterea, pactum quod proedicant, est aperte commentitium et fictum".

The Church's teaching is therefore very clearly formulated on this point and Catholics cannot hesitate to follow it.

Chapter Two

Nature and Purpose of Civil Society

The Nature of Civil Society

Civil society is a natural, necessary, perfect, and organic society. It is natural, which does not only mean that it conforms to the nature of man and that the principles of natural reason are sufficient, in themselves, for its constitution and its functioning; it also implies that its fundamental laws, its essential constitution, are dictated and imposed by nature and that it is not permissible for man to disregard its principles and violate its prescriptions.

Just as, for domestic society, the unity and indissolubility of the marital bond are imposed on men by a superior will, so too, for civil society, there are laws which are imposed on the legislator himself which he does not have the power to break, but which he has the duty to recognize and sanction.

Therefore, not all rights and duties, even in the civil order, derive from human law; the State is not their author and source; but there are imprescriptible rights of which it has a duty to be the protector and guardian. This is why the following proposition was condemned in the Syllabus: 39: the State, as the origin and source of all rights, enjoys a right that is not circumscribed by any limit.

Secondly, civil society is a necessary society, meaning that it is not only in accordance and proportionate to human nature, but that this same nature requires that such a society exist.

What has been said previously about the origin of civil society can serve to prove this necessity and to explain its nature.

The existence of civil society is necessary for the complete and perfect development of the human species; it is not strictly and directly required for the preservation of each individual and each family considered separately.

We will see how important this observation is when we discuss the purpose of society. Civil society is still a perfect society. In the School, a perfect or complete society is defined as one that possesses, within itself, all the means to achieve its purpose, so that it is not destined to find its complement and perfection in a higher society. This is what the

Sovereign Pontiff expressed more briefly in the encyclical *Immortale Dei*, recalling that the Church is a perfect society: "She possesses, within herself and by herself, all the resources necessary for her existence and her activity." Civil society fits this definition of a perfect society well; it possesses all the natural means to provide humankind with the happiness of this life, since in this respect it makes up for everything that is lacking in domestic society; and it is not destined to be part of a higher society of the same order, since we do not see, in the natural order, any society to which it can be subordinated. Thus, civil society is rightly considered a perfect society, and supreme power belongs to it in purely temporal matters.

This is also the teaching of the Holy Father, in the same encyclical; speaking of the two societies, the Church and the State, he says: Each of them, in its own kind, is sovereign.

Finally, civil society is an organic society, meaning that, like living bodies whose members are not animated by purely mechanical movement but each enjoy a life of its own, though dependent on the life of the whole body, civil society is composed of organs whose life and constitution are distinct from its own, while remaining subordinate to it. These vital organs of civil society are its members, that is to say, families, communes, and provinces: for civil society is not composed of individuals, but of lesser societies, prior to it by their nature, more strictly necessary, and more directly instituted by God. These societies have their own rights and constitutions, which civil society has no right to alter or disregard, but which it has a duty to safeguard.

Civil society is therefore not a collection of equal individuals, but a hierarchy of subordinate societies, to which individuals can belong in different capacities and in which they exercise magistracies and functions in relation to their condition.

The constitution of modern societies is far from exhibiting this characteristic; therein lies its fault and its misfortune. Founded for the individual, who recognizes no rights other than individual rights and the rights of the State, this social constitution is inevitably led to oscillate between liberalism and socialism, ultimately falling into complete dissolution. Any definition of civil society that does not present it as a natural, necessary, complete, and hierarchically organized moral body must therefore be rejected. But it is impossible to know the true nature and essential characteristics of civil society without clearly defining its purpose, its end.

The End of Civil Society

It follows from the organic constitution of civil society that its proper and immediate end cannot be the individual good of each man, nor the private good of each family, but the common good of families and other associations which are subordinate to it.

This common good is a temporal good: for the spiritual good is the proper end of the Church, and it cannot be assigned as an immediate goal to civil society without bringing about an inevitable and disastrous confusion between the two powers; it is also an external good: for the internal good, even temporal, of each man is of an individual and private order, not at all of a social order; finally, this temporal good which the union of families in a perfect society should procure consists in public order and prosperity.

This order and prosperity cannot be limited to the mere material conditions of life, and must extend to the entire moral order; indeed, human happiness, even in this life, does not consist solely, or even primarily, in the satisfaction of bodily needs; it depends above all on the intellectual and moral dispositions of the soul. Civil society would therefore not be a natural and perfect society in its order, nor even a truly human society, if it did not strive to provide temporal happiness in accordance with human nature in its highest and most properly human aspects.

Society must therefore provide, by means proportionate to its nature, for the intellectual and moral development of humankind.

If we want to encompass in a single definition the full extent of the purpose of civil society, we will therefore say: Civil society aims at the temporal common good of all man, insofar as this good can be obtained through external actions.[1]

Thus, to assign to society the protection of the rights and freedom of each individual, or the maintenance of public peace and security, is to give an incomplete and truncated definition of its purpose; it must aim to procure the temporal good of man in all its fullness and extent, but only in public order and outside the sphere of action of individuals, families or associations.

Thus, the role of society is very broad: it encompasses everything related to human happiness and self-improvement in this life, but its limits are very clearly defined, since its purpose and mission cease where those of the family and other organs of the social body begin. This conception of the purpose of civil society alone allows us to remain equidistant between the two most formidable pitfalls in these matters: liberalism and socialism.

Chapter Three

Civil Power

The End of Civil Power

It is impossible to conceive of a human society without a visible authority to govern it. Indeed, to form a social body, the multitude of men must not only be united by the knowledge and desire for a common good, but this union must translate into a universal and constant order in the choice of means, the distribution of responsibilities, and the allocation of offices, so that the general good is properly and effectively procured.

However, the difficulty of knowing in practice what is currently beneficial to the common good in given circumstances; the diversity of interests and aptitudes, renders individuals incapable of spontaneously and alone ensuring that society achieves the goal for which it was instituted: a force, an active principle, is therefore needed to prevent the multitude from dividing and dissolving and to constantly bring it back to unity.[1] This is not a question of mechanical unity, that would be the negation of all society, but of a moral and organic unity, whose principle preserves life in each part of the body and, at the same time, coordinates and directs each, according to its nature, to make it serve the good of the whole.

In short, we need someone whose common good is precisely their own good, and who can represent and defend it in the conflict of private interests.

This is the raison d'être of social power.

The Nature of Civil Power

Since the union of men in society is a moral union, social power, in order to achieve its goal, must have the power to bind morally, that is to say, to impose an obligation on the human will, to restrict the legitimate use of its freedom, to demand obedience: the force of social power therefore consists in a right; physical constraint is not the bond that holds men in society, it is a social force only if it is put at the service of the right.

This right to impose an obligation on the will of man constitutes authority. This is why there can be no authority that does not come from God; for no one, by himself, has the power to bind the will of another: God alone essentially possesses this right, God alone can communicate it to men.

This applies to all companies, without exception.

As for civil society, in particular, authority is all the more necessary because its purpose is complex and encompasses the entire temporal order; its members are numerous, their circumstances differ, and their private interests are often opposed.[2] For this society, authority consists in the right to demand obedience from its members to the social power in all that is necessary to achieve the common good, without harming the interests of a higher order. Finally, civil authority, like all others, comes from God.

This is a dogma of faith; it is the formal teaching of the Church, contained very clearly in Holy Scripture; one could not reject this doctrine without falling into heresy. Neither a part nor the whole of society is the source and principle of civil authority; Article 6 of the Declaration of the Rights of Man is therefore in direct opposition to faith.[3]

The Origin of Civil Power

How does God communicate authority to civil society?

Gallicans and Anglicans agreed that royal authority was of direct and immediate divine origin, without any participation from human will. This doctrine aimed to place civil power on a par, in a sense, with ecclesiastical power; the temporal sovereign, holding his authority no less directly from God than the Pope, could claim to be independent of the power of the Vicar of Jesus Christ. Thus, contemporary theologians, whenever they addressed the origin of civil power, endeavored to demonstrate that at the birth of societies, a historical fact arising from circumstances or the will of men, had determined the form of power and the subject of authority.

The modern error of popular sovereignty has led Catholic theologians and philosophers of our time to insist, on the contrary, on the divine origin of civil authority; but, in reality, there are not two doctrines, there are only two ways of defending the same truth.

The common teaching of the doctors is that men, driven by the needs of their nature, come together in society; their will is usually influenced by traditions, circumstances of place, time and people, and even by the action of constraint, and thus determines itself to adopt such a form of government and to recognize such a subject as the holder of social authority; but the power of man cannot go beyond this, he determines the form of power and the subject who must exercise it, he does not create the authority.

This doctrine, more clearly affirmed by modern theologians, is nevertheless found in its entirety among their ancestors of the School.[4]

Theologians use a very apt comparison to explain this: authority is to society what the soul is to man; it is authority that gives society being and life. Authority comes directly from God, just as the soul is the result of a creative action of divine omnipotence; but, just as God creates the human soul when the body has reached a state of formation that makes it capable of being united with it, so too he confers authority on civil society when the latter is sufficiently constituted to present a subject capable of receiving it and exercising its functions.

Authority, therefore, does not always originate from the people, nor does it reside primarily in them; those who hold it are neither their agents nor their representatives. But neither is it directly instituted by God in its concrete form and its existence in a specific person or category of citizens. God alone created our souls, but he did not give us life without the help of our parents; so it is, in proportion, with civil power.

We are now touching on the most delicate part of our subject, and its extreme importance obliges us to give, in more detail, the doctrine of theologians on this question.

We will focus primarily on expounding Suarez's theory on the origin of civil power; firstly, because this illustrious theologian is the faithful interpreter of the teachings of the School; secondly, because his opinion is usually distorted and presented in the most inaccurate way and in the most contrary way to the principles of which he is the defender.

It was in his treatise on Laws, and in his response to King James I of England, that Suarez dealt with the origin of civil power.

In the first work, he studies, as a theologian and philosopher, the principle and nature of legislative power in society.

The response to King James is a polemical work, in which Suarez refutes the errors of the heretical king, particularly on the rights and origins of royal power.

It is in this second work, one can easily understand, that the human side of civil authority is highlighted above all; also, it is rather in the responses to the king's objections against his thesis that Suarez affirms the character and origin of political power.

These two books thus complement each other and show us a great mind, a first-rate theologian, presenting, in its dual aspect, the traditional doctrine of Saint Thomas and the Scholastics.

As a first principle in this matter, and as a truth of faith, Suarez formulates this assertion: "It is just and very much in accordance with human nature that there should be civil magistrates, having temporal authority to govern men."

The second principle, which is not of faith but is certain for reason, is this: "The civil magistrate, if he is sovereign in the temporal order, has the power to make laws in this order, that is to say civil laws, and this by virtue of natural law, provided that he observes the other conditions necessary for justice and the validity of laws."

But whether there are authorities among men with the power to command is another matter entirely, as is defining what those authorities are.

Some jurists and the King of England claimed that authority existed, by divine right, in a particular prince, who then transmitted it by succession.

The certain and common opinion of the doctors, says Suarez, is that "natural law does not attribute political power to any particular man, but to the perfect society as a whole."[5]

It must be said: to the perfect society, and not simply to the multitude, for a confused crowd, which is not formed into a social body, does not possess authority; whereas, on the contrary, men cannot associate themselves, in a political body, without an authority resulting from the very fact of their union.[6]

Does this authority come directly from God, as the author of nature?

Yes, replies Suarez, and this is the true and common doctrine; so that men only arrange the matter and prepare a subject capable of receiving that form which God gives to the social body, by conferring authority upon it.[7]

However, this assertion has two parts that Suarez distinguishes as follows:

The first, that authority comes from God, the first and principal cause; this is clear and certain; the second, that God immediately confers authority; this needs to be explained.[8] Here is the explanation of the learned doctor.

God does not confer authority upon man through a special action, distinct from the creation or preservation of beings, but rather gives it as an inherent property of human nature, when it reaches the full development of its being through the formation of a social body. Indeed, when society is formed, reason alone suffices to show us that God could not have left it devoid of this social power, which is indispensable to its existence.[9]

Therefore, God gave civil authority to political society, just as he gave paternal authority to domestic society.

It is a germ that is in human nature, not in the individual, and that sprouts at the very moment when human intelligence, pressed by necessity, recognizes its existence.

Thus, authority does not reside in isolated individuals; nor does it reside in the confused and disunited multitude; first, a political body must be formed which is its subject.

As soon as it is formed, natural reason recognizes authority, for it is its form. This is what Suarez means when he says that authority is a property, an attribute, which results from the very nature of the social body, once constituted. Human will plays no part: nature and Providence have provided for everything, and it is in this sense that it is true to say: authority comes directly from God.[10]

But here is a remark of the highest importance, and which alone would suffice to distinguish Suarez's doctrine from the opinions which tend to recognize the revolutionary dogma of national sovereignty.

Although sovereign power is a natural property of the perfect society and results from its existence, it is not inalienable; and, either by its consent or by any other legitimate means, the community can be deprived of sovereign power and see it transferred to another subject.[11] This, says Suarez, is a constant truth of reason and experience which results precisely from the fact that the form of political power is not determined by natural or divine law.

Society can be prince of its independence by violence or by a just war; it can give itself to a man or to a city; moreover, natural reason shows "not only that it is not necessary but that it is not in accordance with nature to leave Sovereignty to the whole community," for it could not exercise it.[12]

Sovereignty, therefore, exists in a radical sense within the entire social body, but it is not an inalienable and irrevocable property of that body; indeed, it cannot be properly exercised by it, and it is not in accordance with its nature that it should remain its subject. This is Suarez's doctrine, as it emerges not from a hasty reading or from truncated texts, but from a serious and faithful analysis of his writings. We have followed, with precision, the development of his thought, in the very order in which he presents it, and the pages just read are a summary and often a literal translation of his treatise on the Laws, to which, moreover, everyone can refer. It follows from this doctrine, (we begin again to quote here the text of Suarez) "that civil power, whenever it resides in a man or in a prince, regularly and ordinarily emanates from the people and the community either indirectly or immediately, and that it cannot be legitimately possessed without this."[13]

This is the text invoked by Father Maumus in support of national sovereignty; however, to make the proof more striking, the author omitted the words: mediately or immediately and translated: "Civil power, which by legitimate and ordinary right resides in such a man or in such a prince, emanates from the people. The consent of the nation is the sole source of just power."[14]

This mediate and indirect emanation, mentioned here by Suarez, is however not of minor importance, for it could have served to distinguish the doctrine of the Catholic theologian from the errors of the social contract.

Here, indeed, are the developments between Suarez, concerning this indirect designation of the sovereign by the people.

Royal power, he says, can belong to someone by right of birth; but heredity presupposes the legitimate power of the predecessor, and one thus goes back to a first King, who, for his part, did not succeed anyone; he therefore received his power from the social body and his successors thus hold their power mediately and radically from the people.[15]

Kingship, Suarez continues, can still be established by right of conquest; but the war must be just for the domination to be legitimate. If the war is unjust, it does not establish the right, unless, subsequently, the people accept the usurper. If the war is just, the conquest is a punishment for the people, and then they are obliged to accept the conqueror. Thus, the consent of the people is always involved, but the examples cited show how tacit and indirect this consent is and how it differs from a plebiscite or any other manifestation of national sovereignty.[16]

The Determination of the Subject of Authority

It remains for us to see how Suarez explains this transmission of sovereign power, by which authority, originally spread throughout the social body, like the soul in the body of man, becomes localized, in a way, as the higher faculties of the soul centralize their action in the brain.

This is still about legislative power, an essential attribute of sovereign power; Suarez examines which subject receives the power to make laws directly from God. It is obviously the same as the one who receives sovereign authority directly from God: it is the perfect community. But this follows from the conclusion that those who make laws do not ordinarily derive their power directly from God, "for it is rare, if not unheard of, for the nation to reserve this right for itself and exercise it directly on its own."[17] Are princes, then, merely representatives and agents of the popular legislator?

Let us listen to Suarez's response: if he accepts this hypothesis, he recognizes the sovereignty of the people and the modern constitutional regime; if he rejects it, by what right does he claim to be his authority? We translate literally:

"Here we must distinguish two ways of possessing authority; that is to say, that it can be ordinary or delegated: the authority which comes directly from God and resides in the community is an ordinary authority and it is as such that it is transmitted to the prince by the people, so that he may use it as his own property (ut tanquam proprius dominus illa utatur), and as an essential attribute of his office, (et ut habens illam ex vi proprii muneris)."[18]

Thus, as soon as there is a constituted authority, as soon as power is entrusted to the prince, the people are no longer sovereign, and the prince is master, by virtue of his office, of making laws in his own name. This is stated even more explicitly a few lines later.

A theologian who argued that the representative of an authority could not delegate it to others concluded that princes, not holding their authority directly from God alone, but indirectly through the people, could not delegate their powers to inferior magistrates.

Suarez condemns this doctrine as false: "If it concerns the Emperor, kings, and other princes," he says, "to whom this power of society has been transmitted, this doctrine is false because, for these princes, legislative power is not delegated but ordinary, for they possess it in perpetuity, and it belongs to them by virtue of their office." And here is an even more categorical assertion: "This is why this transmission of powers from society to the prince is not a delegation, but an alienation, a complete abandonment of all the power that was in the community."[19]

We ask the impartial reader to meditate on these texts and tell us what remains in their mind of the legend of Suarez, a supporter of national sovereignty.

For us, it seems that he could rather be accused of having suggested to Louis XIV the famous formula: "I am the State." A formula, moreover, which has a true meaning and is perfectly in accordance with Catholic doctrine, if we designate by the word State the only sovereign power; it is, in fact, the King who is the only sovereign, it is he who possesses in his own right, and to the exclusion of all others, the superior rights of the perfect society, by virtue of this donation, this perfecta largitio of all the political power of the social body which is found at the first origin of monarchies.

Chapter Four

The Best Form of Government

We have thus far been committed to following Suarez's teaching step by step, mainly concerning the origin of civil power, because this doctor is the one most often invoked to cover modern errors with an apparent conformity to the doctrine of the Church.

The question we are now addressing is one of those on which there is no appearance of disagreement among theologians or philosophers; we will therefore follow, in treating it, the prince of doctrine, Saint Thomas Aquinas, and we will show by some quotations what the other doctors think with him.

In his treatise entitled: On the King and the Kingdom, after defining the king: "He who governs, for the common good, the people of a city or a province."[1] Saint Thomas Aquinas examines whether it is more advantageous for the city or the State to be governed by several or by one.

To answer this question, the holy doctor says, we must study what good society expects from its government. The good that the multitude expects from those who govern it is that kind of unity called peace; a good without which society becomes more harmful than useful. Therefore, the more a government is capable of maintaining the unity of peace in society, the better it is. "Now, it is evident that what is one, by itself, is more suited to producing unity than what is many; likewise, what is hot, by its nature, is most suited to warming; the government of one is therefore better than that of many."[2]

This is not enough; Saint Thomas amasses proofs drawn from common sense and experience. "It is evident," he says, "that the multitude cannot be well governed by many if those many are divided among themselves. For there must be a certain unity among many in order for them to be able to govern in anything; but union among many exists only by analogy to that which is one in itself; therefore, that which is one in itself governs better."[3]

Next comes the proof from experience: here is how it is developed by Saint Thomas:

"States and cities not governed by one person are torn apart by factions and shaken by discord, as if to fulfill the complaints of the Lord through his prophet. (Jeremiah 12:10) On the contrary, states and cities governed by one person enjoy peace, flourish in justice, and prosper in abundance. Therefore, the Lord promises his people, through the prophet, as an excellent gift, that he will place a leader at their head and that one prince will reign over them."[4]

It was not the theologians of the Middle Ages and the Renaissance who invented this doctrine; it was the philosophers of antiquity, citizens of the free cities of Greece and Asia Minor, who taught, with the authority of reason and experience, the superiority of monarchy over every other legitimate form of government. It was by commenting on Aristotle that Saint Thomas and Suarez rediscovered the doctrine founded, above, on the testimony of the Holy Scriptures.[5]

One objection still needs to be addressed.

If the government of one is the best, because it is stronger to unite the various elements of the social body, this government will be the worst of all, if the one who commands is bad.

Saint Thomas agrees; he sets forth this thesis in a long chapter (chapter III), the conclusion of which is this: idem videtur, tyranno subjici et bestae soevienti substerni "It is because monarchy is at once the best and the worst of governments that many hate kings, because of the malice of tyrants; others, on the contrary, because they regret kingship, give themselves over to the cruelty of a despot; and many govern as tyrants under the pretext of reigning as kings... There is therefore peril on both sides: either that, out of fear of tyranny, one avoids monarchy, which is the best government; or that, out of love for it, one gives oneself over to a monarchy that becomes tyrannical."[6]

We will certainly not be accused of truncating the texts, or of passing over in silence those that might seem contrary to our doctrines. What Saint Thomas, a resolute supporter of monarchy, may have said, cannot, moreover, harm the thesis we defend after him. As with Suarez, we quote everything, and we faithfully follow the chain of proofs and thoughts of the holy Doctor. After weighing, with the impartiality of a great mind, the advantages and disadvantages of the monarchical regime, he continues: "When, of two things, each of which has its dangers, one must necessarily be chosen, the one that entails the fewest evils must have our preference. Now, when the monarchy degenerates into tyranny, fewer evils result than from an aristocratic government if it degenerates into an oligarchy; for discord, a frequent consequence of the rule of many, is the opposite of peace, that supreme good of the social body; whereas tyranny does not destroy the peace but only jeopardizes the property of a few individuals, unless it becomes excessive and attacks the entire multitude. Therefore, the government of one must still be preferred to that of many, although both have their dangers.[7]

But let us quote again: "It is more common for the people to face extreme dangers under the rule of many than under that of one. For it easily happens that among several, someone ceases to strive for the common good. Now, if even one of those who govern ceases to provide for the good of society, the danger of discord becomes imminent, because the discord of the leaders inevitably leads to that of the people; if, on the contrary, there is only one leader: first, most often, he applies himself to providing for the public good; and when he loses interest in it, it does not immediately follow that he oppresses his subjects, which is the ultimate degree of tyranny... Moreover, it is no less rare to see the rule of many turn into oppression; indeed, this may even be more frequent." Indeed, when discord arises where there are several leaders, it often happens that one of them rises above the others and usurps the dominion of the multitude for himself alone. History provides clear examples of this. For almost always, the rule of many results in the tyranny of one, as was seen especially in the Roman Republic...

"Thus, since the fear of tyranny would be the strongest reason for rejecting the best of all forms of government; and since tyranny is no less frequent, on the contrary, under the government of many than under that of one, it follows that it is simply better to live under a king than to live in a republic."[8]

This language is timeless because it is the highest expression of truth and common sense. But is there no way to preserve a monarchical government from the peril of tyranny and thus raise it one step higher, above the government of many?

It is Saint Thomas who will answer us once again:

"First, those to whom this duty falls must raise to the throne a man such that he cannot appear inclined to tyranny.

"Secondly, the government of the kingdom must be constituted in such a way that the king, once established, finds no pretext for tyranny.

"Thirdly, its power must be tempered, so that it cannot easily degenerate into tyranny...

"Finally, if the king tyrannizes, it is necessary to provide for preventing him from doing so."[9] What is this political organization and this temperament of royal power intended to prevent tyranny?

We find an overview of this in the Summa Theologica. (Prim. Sec. quest. CV, art. I.) "The best form of government is that of a city or kingdom where a single virtuous ruler is placed above all, having below him several virtuous princes; nevertheless, all participate in this government, either because the princes can be chosen from among the people, or even because they are chosen by the people. For such is all well-constituted political power: it partakes of kingship insofar as one single ruler presides; of aristocracy, insofar as several virtuous men participate in the government; of democracy, that is to say, of popular power, insofar as men of the people can be chosen as leaders and it belongs to the people to appoint them."

Saint Thomas, immediately applying this theory to the constitution of the Hebrew people, shows us in Moses the monarch whose sovereign authority gives the government the form of kingship; in the seventy-two elders the aristocratic element of power in that they are chosen by God from among the wise, and the democratic element in those who are designated by the people.[10] This example completes the explanation and clarification of the thought of the holy doctor. (Prim. Sec. q. CV. a. 1). Here, on the other hand, is the commentary of Cardinal Zigliara:

"Monarchy is tempered," he said, "when the king is bound by certain fundamental laws of the kingdom that limit his power and, moreover, when he cannot make laws without the assistance of certain second-ranking dignitaries, for example, the governors of cities and provinces or their delegates, and when he is required to ask for and obtain their consent."[11] Cardinal Zigliara did not consider this form of monarchy the only legitimate one, but he defined it in opposition to absolute monarchy, where the king is bound neither by fundamental laws that he has promised to observe, nor by the obligation of his council's consent.

This, according to the doctrine of all theologians, is the best form of government. It is noteworthy that it makes no mention of national sovereignty, universal suffrage, or elected legislative assemblies. Instead, it is the high-ranking officials of the state who advise the king and give their consent to his laws. Their role is not to represent the people, nor are they necessarily elected by them; they inform the prince about the situation in his provinces and defend the particular interests of those they are charged with governing, in his name.

We will see later the importance of these remarks, in relation to the subject and exercise of legislative power.

PART II
REVOLUTIONARY DOCTRINE

Chapter Five

The Principles

While the Church's doctrine on political matters is little known, one is sure to find the reader initiated into all the errors and doctrines whose formidable combination is the true cause of the triumph of the Revolution.

Therefore, in this second part of our work, we will not attempt to provide a detailed and documented exposition of revolutionary doctrine; we will quickly recall its principles, which are, alas! present in everyone's minds, and we will highlight what is most directly contrary to Catholic doctrine in them.

There have been discord and civil wars among all peoples; there have been revolts, even revolutions, throughout history; we saw them before 1789; we have seen almost as many since then as in the entire course of centuries. Yet there is only one Revolution.

When we say "the Revolution," no one asks whether we are referring to the events that took place in England, Germany, or Switzerland; whether we are referring to the movements of 1830, 1848, or 1871; our thoughts immediately turn, without hesitation, to the terrible period at the end of the eighteenth century. What then comes to mind is not merely a confused collection of events; the succession of years that make up the period of revolutionary violence; but a specific date, even more infamous for the magnitude of its errors than it deserves to be for the magnitude of its crimes: the year 1789, the year of the dogmatic definition of the principles of the Revolution.

Why is that?

Because the principles of social, political, and religious order proclaimed in 1789 contained within them the entire Revolution, that is to say, the complete and radical upheaval of religion, family, and society. You look to the future with anxiety, you consider the rising tide of human errors and passions, and you wonder what the world will be like if this torrent is not stopped; but consider that these men whose actions you fear, and he goes into minute detail about the reasons that must determine the choice of location for the capital city and even for the kingdom. These are therefore exceptional circumstances that are encountered only at the origin of a monarchy.

You fear the application of socialist theories; but let modern industry take its course, let the economic system created by the Revolution take its course, let the secularized State, monopolizing the wealth of citizens, take its course, and agree that the socialists will have to hurry if they want to find something else to destroy.

Chapter Six

Sovereignty of Man

What then is the Revolution? The fundamental dogma of the Revolution is this: Man is born free and independent by nature.

This is an absolute freedom, a complete independence, which is essential to human nature and, consequently, inalienable. Everything that emanates from the free will of man is good, is sacred; no external force has the power, the right, to obstruct it: that would be a crime against humanity. However, it is impossible for all wills to simultaneously enjoy this complete exercise of their freedom, which is a right; people need to live in society, and to live in society, they must yield to one another, they must submit to leaders.

How can this inevitable submission be reconciled with the absolute independence of man?

Here it is:

It is assumed that society exists only by virtue of a pact, a contract, the social contract.

Men, all sovereign, all independent, said to themselves: we must come together in society, and since there cannot be a society without leaders, we will make, we will create leaders.

How so?

We are sovereign each of ourselves and ourselves alone; let us pool this sovereignty; let us designate someone among us to be the custodian of this sum of sovereignty and to exercise it in our name, as long as we permit him to exercise it, in this way someone will direct society towards its end, and yet, in obeying him, each will only obey himself.

As we can see, God has nothing to do with any of this.

Who is governed? The people.

Who governs? The people.

Where does authority come from? From the people.

He is sovereign; he is so by nature, by essence; he cannot not be, he cannot renounce his sovereignty.

Why? Because each man, each of these millions of individuals, is his own sovereign; his will is queen and mistress, it is its own law; there is no power outside of it that has the right to impose laws upon him, that is to say, limits, a barrier, a restraint. There is only one limit to the freedom of each man: not to hinder the freedom of others, because all men are equal, equally free, equally sovereign. Thus, wherever one turns to seek a moderator and a master, one finds only one, always the same: man, and nothing but him.

There is no longer a moral law imposed by nature, there is no longer a divine law revealed by God, there is no longer a God in human society; it is secularized, laicized. That is why we only speak of human rights and not of human duties.

Thus the law is only "the expression of the general will",[1] of the human will and not of the will of God; "the source of all authority resides essentially in the nation,"[2] and not in the one who judges the nations, because the people, that is to say man, have taken the place of the Creator; he is free, he is sovereign, he is God.

That is the final word of the Revolution.

Therefore, as soon as God appears in the world, as soon as his name is spoken anywhere or his representatives raise their voices, the Revolution cries out: there is the enemy! The war is without truce and without mercy between the Revolution and those who have remained faithful to God on earth, because the Revolution is an attempt to organize the world without God and against God, it is satanic in its essence.

This is the most tremendous mistake; it is TOTAL HERESY.

Heresy, in that it denies the dependence of each man and of society on God and his law.

Heresy, in that it assumes that sovereignty is inherent in man and that authority does not come immediately from God, which is a dogma of faith.

Finally, it is an error in that it imagines an impossible and illusory social contract that delivers men to the worst kind of tyranny, by promising them sovereignty.

Here, on this subject, are words taken from the Encyclical on the Christian Constitution of States.

"Those who want civil society to have originated from the free choice of the will of men," says the Pope, "derive authority from the same source. Each person, they say, has relinquished a portion of their sovereignty to voluntarily place themselves under the power of the one in whom the sum of all rights, thus alienated, would be found."

"It is a great mistake not to see that men, not being a savage race, are made by nature to live in society.

"Furthermore, this social pact, which they advocate, is manifestly false and supposed.

"It cannot provide the political power with the strength, prestige and stability necessary to defend society and provide for the well-being of its members.

"This splendor and these guarantees are found together only where sovereignty is considered to emanate from the most great and most holy God."[3]

Chapter Seven

Liberty

The fundamental error of the Revolution, as we have seen, was to place man in the place of God. It did not deny God's existence; it went further, it took his place in the world, and as soon as anyone tries to reinstate him, it protests furiously as if against an invader. But if the Revolution had openly displayed itself in this way and proclaimed this pretension, it would have aroused public reason and conscience; it needed a mask, it needed a deceptive program to seduce and sway people, a word, an idea that seemed grand and beautiful to them, and for which they would be capable of sacrificing everything.

What is this word? Freedom!

Freedom was not a new thing in the world, it could not be new in a society steeped in Christianity, and especially among this noble and chivalrous French nation which, for more than a thousand years, had waged war across the world in defense of noble causes and the liberation of the oppressed.

What was new was the false idea we had of freedom.

Here is the revolutionary idea of freedom:

"Freedom consists in being able to do anything that does not harm others."

At first glance, this definition seems fair and harmless: that is precisely what makes it dangerous. Being able to do anything that does not harm others means that we only have duties towards other people. Towards God and towards ourselves—that is, towards God's law which governs our innermost actions—there are none.

Blasphemy, sacrilege, and impiety, as long as they do not infringe upon the freedom of others, are things that the law can neither prevent nor repress.

Drunkenness, debauchery, suicide attempts, all these are acts that the moralist can condemn, but that society cannot defend as long as a third party is not harmed.

What she respects is man, but not man's honor and dignity, only his freedom.

She alone is sacred.

And if the Christian sense of the people did not prevent the principle from reaching its ultimate consequences, every crime, every outrage committed against the human person, with the consent of that person, should remain unpunished.

You do not have the right to use threats or violence to impose your opinions on others or to make them abandon their beliefs.

Is it because their beliefs are good and your opinions are bad? We hardly give such a trifle a thought.

It is solely out of respect for liberty; therefore, leave this liberty to itself, and through specious books, skillful lies, an appearance of truth, a display of erudition, and witty pronouncements, spread doubt, darkness, and ignorance in souls, corrupt morals, pervert hearts—what does it matter to the Revolution? You have exercised your liberty by leaving your victims to choose between the evil you offer them and the good you conceal from them: Long live liberty!

That is revolutionary freedom.

True freedom, on the contrary, is the reasonable use that man makes of his will, in accordance with the law of God and the just laws of men.

The power to do evil is a weakness and a corruption of freedom. To take it away or restrict it is to liberate it.

Chapter Eight

Equality

Alongside the word liberty, there is another that the Revolution placed in the first article of its credo, at the beginning of the Declaration of Rights: Equality.

"Men are born and remain free and equal in rights."

Having proclaimed the sovereign independence of man, the Revolution, during the century that is ending, has spelled out on the bloody pages of our history the word LIBERTY; it is preparing to teach us, during the century to come, what EQUALITY means.

Just as there is true freedom, there is also true equality between men, either from the point of view of nature or from the point of view of grace.

All men are equal by nature; this simply means that all men are men. They all have an immortal soul and a mortal body; they all have the capacity to reason and to will; there is among them this equality which necessarily exists between individuals of the same species.

Moreover, there is a supernatural equality among all people. All are redeemed by Jesus Christ; for each of us, He shed His blood. Here again, equality is complete. Every person is worth the blood of the only Son of God.

If the Revolution had said nothing different, it would have remained true; it would not have been the Revolution. But in its view, equality is a necessary consequence of the autonomy and sovereign independence of man.

Therefore, in 1789, she proclaimed the absolute equality of rights.

These rights, equal for all, are freedom, they are the sovereignty of man over himself, by virtue of which he recognizes no other law than his will, no other duty than that of not submitting to anyone and of not doing anything to others, good or bad, except by persuasion.

This is the new law. It is the same for everyone, equal for all, sovereign in all, because it is not only a human right, but a divine one.

It is pointless to refute revolutionary theory with arguments based on the necessary inequality of men and conditions; the Revolution did not deny this, but it affirmed that man is without a master and it made all equal by proclaiming their sovereignty.

There is one man to whom the Church recognizes this sovereign right, only one, and that is the God-Man, Our Lord Jesus Christ, because his human reason and will, personally united to the divine nature, are truly the reason and will of a God.

There is one man, and one only, to whom the Revolution does not recognize these sovereign rights, and that is the God-Man, because his living humanity is no longer visible to our eyes, he has lost the right to be counted as a part of the people.

Like God, he is nothing.

O terrible war of the rebellious man!

IMPERET ILLI DEUS!

Chapter Nine

Revolutionary Form of Government

Catholic doctrine is compatible with all forms of government. Since "all power comes from God," it can derive from this primary source either from the people, which is the republic; or from the hands of several, which is the aristocracy, another form of the republic; or from the hands of one, which is the monarchy.

In each of these political constitutions, it is recognized that those who govern are God's representatives and represent only God. This is self-evident in aristocracies and monarchies. The same is true in the People's Republic; if there is an authority that commands, even if elected, it commands in the name of God.

This cannot be the case with revolutionary doctrine. The source of all authority resides essentially in the nation.

The multitude is the natural and necessary subject of public power; it cannot validly alienate it.

Government must therefore be democratic; this is a natural right; any other form of power cannot be legitimate.

We say that the government must necessarily be democratic, however it may not always be republican.

Two political forms are compatible with revolutionary democracy: the constitutional monarchy and the parliamentary republic. Aristocracy is not an option, because the two preceding forms differ from each other only in one respect: the duration of the head of state's powers and the method of their transfer.

Therefore, in reality, there is only one political regime, if not one form of government, that is compatible with revolutionary doctrine. And, in fact, wherever revolutionary doctrine has prevailed—that is to say, throughout the entire civilized world—it has established this regime, beginning by imposing it on the old monarchies, then founding new ones, and gradually replacing them with republics.

Thus, contrary to the doctrine of the church, which, while recognizing the theoretical superiority of royalty, also admits other forms as good and legitimate, provided they are justly established and honestly practiced, the revolutionary doctrine ultimately admits only one political regime, and it proclaims it imposed by the NEW LAW.

This is the system of REPRESENTATIVE GOVERNMENT.

Here are the principles and constituent elements of this regime.[1]

The representative system rests entirely on the principle of national sovereignty. The sovereign people govern themselves through their representatives.

If there is a king, he reigns but does not govern. Between him and the people, a pact has been concluded; this is the constitution, which only the sovereign people can modify, in agreement with the king.

It is the people who govern through their elected representatives, to whom they delegate the legislative power of which they are the source and the necessary subject. They make the laws in their name.

These representatives make up what is called the nation's Legislative Body or Parliament. In some countries, the king himself chooses senators who form another Chamber, also legislative, to counterbalance the influence of the first; but the existence of this second Chamber is not essential to the representative system.

Laws made by the Legislative Body are signed by the Head of State and executed by the ministers. These ministers are chosen by the head of the executive branch and are responsible to Parliament for the implementation of the laws.

The Chambers can overthrow the ministry by refusing it what is called a vote of confidence.

If the head of state cannot find ministers who are in line with his policy and have the confidence of the Chambers, he has the right to dissolve the Chamber of Deputies and the duty to call upon the people, within a period fixed by the Constitution, to express their will through new elections.

Just as the executive and legislative powers are divided and delegated by the people to different subjects, so too is the judicial power, another essential attribute of sovereignty, divided into two bodies, one of which judges the law, which is the magistracy, and the other judges the fact, which is the jury.

Finally, to guarantee the people the exercise of their sovereignty, they are granted the right to write and speak against the government, that is, the members of parliament and the ministers. To ensure some respect for the head of state, he is declared immune from prosecution by the Constitution.

Thus, the sovereignty of the people, the division of powers between the head of the executive, the legislative body, the judiciary and the jurors, the recourse to national consultation in case of conflicts, this is the essential mechanism of the revolutionary regime of representative government.

As we can see, in this system, the republic and the monarchy differ only in the duration and the mode of transmission of executive power. In a monarchy, the head of state is not elected and his power is hereditary; in a republic, the president is elected by the Chambers for a given term.[2] Finally, in a third form, that of the plebiscitary monarchy, executive power is both hereditary and elective, meaning that the monarch, then called the "Emperor," comes to power by inheritance or by surprise, and then has his possession ratified by the vote of the people.

These are differences that do not alter the essence of the representative system. They arose from circumstances and served to allow for the gradual introduction of the principles and institutions of revolutionary government where it was not possible to immediately detach the people from the princes in whom they placed their trust. Conversely, where people could be separated from their sovereigns, the republic was everywhere established as the form that best corresponded to these principles of government. We can, and indeed must, disregard the various forms, or rather the different names, of the representative system in order to study it in its essence and critique it in the light of the teachings of reason and faith.

This study, we hope, will shed some light on the present situation of French Catholics, by showing the place that can be left to legitimate political disagreements and the truths that must unite all minds and hearts in a common hatred of the revolution and its works.

PART III
REASON AND FAITH

Chapter Ten

Judgement of Theologians

For them, every government, however popular it might be supposed to be, was the representative of God, not the agent of the people, and if, by some impossible chance, they had been told that power, while coming from God, resided essentially in the nation, they would have replied that in principle authority could not reside in the hands of one who is essentially incapable of exercising it by himself, and that in fact, all peoples are governed by princes or political bodies possessing ordinary and sovereign authority, in no way delegated by the nation.

We have seen, in this regard, the decisive text of Suarez, and if history could, from that time, provide some example of democratic government where the people had expressly reserved legislative and sovereign power to themselves, it was an exception, realized in some municipal republic of Italy or Flanders, it was not and could not be the political regime of a great nation.

It is to the theologians of this century that we must ask what the Church thinks of representative government. We will do so by following the doctrine of two illustrious Catholic philosophers, legitimate heirs and faithful interpreters of the great traditions and pure scholastic doctrines: Cardinal Zigliara and Rabbi Liberatore.

The books in which they dealt with these matters are classic works, which serve as a theme for teaching in the main universities of Rome and which give us the authorized doctrine of the great religious orders of Saint Ignatius and Saint Dominic.

By reading them, we are listening to the entire School. We will see, in the next chapter, their perfect conformity with the Encyclicals recently published on the question.

In his assessment of the representative regime, Cardinal Zigliara is, on the surface, more severe than Father Liberatore.

"This form of government," said Liberatore, "although absolutely imperfect, can nevertheless be relatively better than others, and, where it is legitimately established, it obliges citizens to obedience."[1]

"The representative form of government is, of all, the most imperfect," Zigliara says briefly.[2]

Although their terminology differs, the two theologians' thinking is identical. To be certain of this,

JUDGEMENT OF THEOLOGIANS

we need only compare their respective lists of the flaws in this regime. According to Zigliara, the foundation of constitutional government is that legislative power belongs to the people, a doctrine that presupposes popular sovereignty and is the essential condition for the existence of this government. This principle is absurd and anti-social.[3]

Liberatore makes the same criticisms:

"In order for this form of government to provide the public good in a lasting way, it must, he said, be freed from the principal vices found within it."[4]

Now, the vices that Father Liberatore points out in the representative system, and from which he declares it necessary to free it in order for it to procure the public good, which is the very end of a government, are the following:

The foundation of this regime is the sovereignty of the people. This principle is not only false, it is the constant cause of continuous sedition.

Secondly, adds Father Liberatore, public opinion is taken as the rule of government policy. "This principle is destructive of the moral law, which is not founded on public or private opinion, but on the immutable rules of justice; it substitutes for them a shifting criterion that usually results from the clamor of the wicked or the sophisms and lies of a venal press. This amounts to substituting force for right, for what is the majority, in itself, if not force?" As for legislative power, says Zigliara, what power demands more wisdom, honesty, prudence, and knowledge of people, things, and times? Yet, in a representative system, this power belongs to the people, who are denied the competence to exercise it, while being granted the power to choose legislators. Thus, the people elect incompetent or wicked individuals. These individuals, vested with the mandate of popular sovereignty, divide themselves into factions, for or against the ministry, and laws are passed amidst divisions and intrigues, with "insane haste" and revolting partiality. "So that, often, it is no longer a legislative assembly, but a tyrannical council, resulting in incredible oppression for the people."[5]

Father Liberatore shares this sentiment, viewing the separation of powers as a constant source of sedition and intrigue, incompatible with the peace that authority must guarantee to society. The theologians whose doctrine we have just summarized primarily consider constitutional monarchy, and it is of this that they say: "This form of government, if it is not rid of the vices we have pointed out, does not stand up to scrutiny."[6] What would they have said of our republic and universal suffrage as it functions today?

The illustrious Bishop of Angers, Mgr Freppel, for whom France will long mourn, drew, in his pamphlet on the French Revolution, a masterful picture of the absurdities and perils of the sovereignty of the people and universal suffrage.

"What is inadmissible, from the point of view of common sense, is that, under the pretext of equality, the number alone, operating by its arithmetic virtue and apart from any other consideration, should become the supreme law of a country; that neither talent, nor fortune, nor morality should enter into anything in a calculation that is reduced to a simple addition of votes; that it should be indifferent from the point of view of law, to represent the interests of an entire family, of an entire corporation or to be concerned only with oneself, and that on an election day, where do questions arise in the choice of a representative, what am I saying? "In a form of government, the most difficult questions of constitutional law, of relations with foreign countries, questions of life or death for a people, the vote of an individual who can barely read and write, or who was found in a workhouse, weighs the same in the balance of national destinies as that of a statesman seasoned in affairs by long experience. No sophistry can cloak such absurdity with a specious pretext."[7]

What can we add to these strong and luminous words? There is, however, something more serious and more odious: it is when the question arises of whether a nation will remain Christian or whether it will cease to be so, and when the Constitution of that people leaves to universal suffrage the right to decide in the final instance.

So it is multitudes blinded by passions and prejudices, deceived by the sophisms of politicians, poisoned by millions of filthy sheets who will, in a single day, without discussion, without examination, without any concern for law and justice, decide on the eternal salvation of souls and the eighteen-century existence of the Church in the country.

The Church, for its part, will not even be heard; it has no say in the debate, its voice counts for nothing. If the Bishop, if the priest speaks, it is as citizens. They have the right to vote, along with the Jew and the Freemason. These nameless slips of paper, all equal, all alike, will then be counted, and the number will decide.

No, "there is no sophistry that can color such an absurdity with a specious pretext," such a crime!

Such a system, "if it is not rid of these vices, does not withstand scrutiny."

In the face of this, Catholics must rise up with the full height of their outraged faith and proclaim that their rights are not subject to popular vote or the laws of the State.

It is better to have the people as executioners than to accept them as judges.

Chapter Eleven

Doctrines of the Holy See

The works whose doctrine we summarized in the previous chapter are philosophical treatises. The errors upon which the political constitution of the representative regime rests are not considered there from the perspective of faith. It is to the Holy See itself that we turn for guidance on this crucial part of our work.

This principle of popular sovereignty, which has found its expression in the political institutions of our time and, more than anywhere else, of our country, has been judged by the Church in recent times through the words of the Vicar of Jesus Christ. What judgment has it passed on the entirety of the political institutions founded on the new law and which constitute the revolutionary regime? This is what we will now attempt to explain.

The general rule for the Church's conduct with regard to revolutionary dogmas and institutions is clearly formulated in the eightieth and final condemned proposition of the Syllabus.

"The Roman Pontiff can and must reconcile himself and compromise with progress, liberalism, and modern civilization."

"Romanus Pontifex potest ac debet cum progressu, cum liberalismo et cum recenti civilitate sese reconciliare et componere."

Modern civilization, progress and liberalism, are all things with which there can be neither reconciliation nor compromise.

However, the new law and the current system of national representation, by everyone's admission, are one of the forms, and not the least, of modern civilization, progress and liberalism .

Therefore, for the Church, there is neither conciliation nor possible transaction with such a regime of government.

The tenth proposition condemned in the Syllabus is thus conceived:

"Authority is nothing more than the sum of numbers and material forces."

This is an explicit condemnation of the sovereignty of universal suffrage, whose absolute authority, in representative government, consists solely in "the sum of numbers".

Those who are not convinced by these texts can refer to the Encyclical *Immortale Dei*, on the Christian Constitution of States, where they will read the explicit condemnation of the sovereignty of the people and of the regime which makes those who govern the representatives of the nation.

"As for the sovereignty of the people, which, without any regard for God, is said to reside by natural right in the people, while it is eminently suited to inflame and flatter a multitude of passions, it rests on no solid foundation and cannot have sufficient strength to guarantee public safety and the peaceful maintenance of order. Indeed, under the sway of these doctrines, principles have weakened to such an extent that, for many, it is an imprescriptible law in political law to be able to legitimately incite sedition, for the prevailing opinion is that the heads of government are now merely delegates charged with executing the will of the people; hence the necessary consequence that everything can equally change at the whim of the people and that there is always a risk of unrest."

In another passage of the same Encyclical, the Sovereign Pontiff sets forth "the foundations and principles" of this "new law, hitherto unknown and in more than one respect at odds not only with Christian law but with natural law."

We would not want to subtract or modify anything from this exposition, so we quote it in its entirety; the reader will see in it the most striking confirmation of the doctrine we support.

Here is the first of all these principles: all men, since they are of the same race and the same nature, are alike, and, in fact, equal among themselves in the practice of life; each one is so entirely his own responsibility that he is in no way subject to the authority of another; he can, in complete freedom, think about everything as he pleases, do as he pleases; no one has the right to command others.

"In a society founded on these principles, public authority is only the will of the people, who, depending only on themselves, are also the only ones to govern themselves.

"He chooses his representatives, but in such a way that he delegates to them less the right than the function of power, to exercise it in his name. The sovereignty of God is passed over in silence, exactly as if God did not exist, or did not concern himself at all with the society of humankind, or as if men, either individually or in society, owed nothing to God, or as if one could imagine any power whatsoever whose cause, strength and authority did not reside entirely in God himself."

"In this way, the State is nothing other than the multitude, master and governing itself."[1] After listing the disastrous effects of such doctrines on the condition of societies and the relations between Church and State, the Pope adds:

"These doctrines, which human reason condemns and which have such a considerable influence on the course of public affairs, the Roman Pontiffs, our predecessors, in full awareness of what the Apostolic Office demanded of them, never allowed them to be issued with impunity..."

"From these decisions of the Sovereign Pontiffs it must absolutely be admitted that the origin of public power must be attributed to God and not to the multitude; that the right to riot is repugnant to reason; that disregarding the duties of religion, or treating different religions in the same way, is not permitted to individuals or societies; that the unlimited freedom to think and to express one's thoughts in public should in no way be ranked among the rights of citizens, nor among things worthy of favor and protection."[2]

In the Encyclical *Diuturnum illud* on civil power, the condemnation of the sovereignty of the people is perhaps even more formal.

"Several among the moderns, following in the footsteps of those who, in the last century, called themselves philosophers, claim that omnipotence derives from the people: so that those who have authority in society do not exercise it as if they possessed it themselves, but only as representatives of the people, and on the condition that the same will of the people who entrusted them with this mandate can always take it back from them.

"But Catholics do not accept this doctrine, because they place the origin of the power to command in God, as in his natural and necessary principle."[3]

Finally, placing himself, from both a historical and doctrinal point of view, the Sovereign Pontiff adds:

"Modern theories on political power have caused great harm, and it is to be feared that this harm will reach even the worst extremes in the future. Indeed, to refuse to attribute to God the power to command men is to deprive public authority of all its splendor and strength. By making it dependent on the will of the people, one commits, first of all, a fundamental error, and, moreover, gives authority only a fragile and inconsistent foundation."

Such opinions act as a perpetual stimulant to popular passions, which will grow bolder every day and pave the way for public ruin, opening the door to secret conspiracies and open sedition...

"It is from this heresy (the Reformation) that, in the last century, both false philosophy, and what is called modern law and the sovereignty of the people, and this unbridled license outside of which many can no longer see true freedom."[4]

Thus, the sovereignty of the people is not only a danger to society, a cause of sedition and ruin, it is an error which a Catholic is in no way permitted to admit, because he is of faith, according to the testimony of Scripture, that "all power comes from God".

The sovereignty of the people is a heresy.

The foundation upon which the Revolution built modern political institutions is therefore unacceptable to Catholics.

It is also true for all men of experience and common sense.

Pius IX had said it in the Encyclical *Quanta cura* :

"Some men, disregarding the older principles of sound reason, dare to proclaim that the will of the people, manifested by what they call public opinion or in some other way, constitutes the supreme law, independent of all divine and human right; and that, in the political order, accomplished facts, by the very fact that they are accomplished, have the value of law."

This is a condemnation of the first principles of modern law.

No Catholic, we are convinced, admits national sovereignty in the heretical and absolute sense in which it is condemned by the Church, but are there not some who, without seeing in the people the sole source of authority and the necessary subject in whom it must reside, nevertheless consider that the power, which comes from God, resides, by right, in the nation "which exercises it directly or through its representatives."[5]

If Catholics were content to assert that a nation can, under certain conditions, be constituted in such a way that legislative power belongs to an elected body of representatives of the people, this would be a question of positive law that would not directly engage doctrine.

But they claim that this kind of constitution responds to a "fundamental maxim" on which "our modern public law is based and of which the republic is, or should be, the widest application."[6] They thus pose the question on the ground of principles, and find themselves led to conclude that there are no true public freedoms, nor sufficient guarantees for the independence of a nation, if the powers are not constituted in this way.

But on what basis can such an assertion be supported, if not on the principles condemned by the

Church, of the absolute autonomy and independence of the multitude?

If the nation is not the source of power, why is it that authority cannot cease to reside within it? What practical consequence would the heresy of the sovereignty of the majority have, which is not found in a system where the people are proclaimed the necessary subject of legislative power?

Catholics who adhere to this doctrine undoubtedly differ from rationalists, but only in that they accept the consequence whose principle others have established. Now, if false principles are errors, their consequences are evils, and those who accept the consequences are complicit with those who propagate errors.

We must therefore push back the consequences with principles and deny that power, which comes from God, can only be entrusted to agents, to representatives of the people.

Therefore, we can conclude this chapter with even more certainty than the previous one and repeat the words of R.P. Liberatore: "Such a regime, if it is not rid of such vices, does not withstand scrutiny."

PART IV
CONCLUSION

CHAPTER TWELVE

Theorical Conclusions

It can easily be deduced from the above how futile and disrespectful to the Holy See is the opinion of those who see in the recent Encyclical to the Bishops and Catholics of France a pure and simple acceptance of the political institutions of our country.

Nowhere, indeed, have the sovereignty of the people and the most pernicious errors of modern law and of the Revolution found a more complete expression than in the current Constitution of the government of France; nowhere have they given more rapidly and with a more inexorable logic the measure of the ruins and atrocities that they are likely to accumulate.

It is therefore inconceivable to suppose that the Holy Father, in protesting against the laws of the Republic and recognizing that same Republic as the current government of the country, intended to legitimize or absolve the monstrous flaws of its Constitution. The respect due to constituted powers in no way implies adherence to the Constitution itself, much less to what, in its institutions or principles, is contrary to faith, reason, or justice.

This is all the more certain in the case at hand, since the institutions and principles which we have condemned are not essentially linked to the current form of the French government.

Every government that has succeeded one another in France for the past century has recognized the sovereignty of the people and retained legislative power in the hands of the nation's representatives. Among the monarchies of Europe, Spain, Belgium, Italy, and others also operate under this system of national representation. Therefore, Catholics cannot be accused of obeying political concerns or succumbing to partisanship if they declare that they do not accept the principle of popular sovereignty and wish to entrust legislative power to someone other than the nation's representatives.

"It must be carefully noted here," said the Sovereign Pontiff, "that whatever the form of civil powers in a nation , it cannot be considered so definitive that it must remain immutable, even if that were the intention of those who originally determined it."

That was certainly the intention of those who established the revolutionary institutions of the representative regime in France.

In their eyes, these are natural rights, because without them there are no longer any true public liberties. But this false opinion cannot stop us in any way; we must, in conscience and as Catholics, loudly condemn the disastrous principle of popular sovereignty; we must remember that the right to decide the future and religion of the country belongs neither to the electoral college nor to its representatives, but that the French nation is bound to Christ by a fourteen-century-old covenant that no power can break.

This is what is imposed on the conscience of every French Catholic.

On other points, there is room for legitimate differences of opinion. Regarding the question of which is the best form of government, considered in itself or in relation to the customs and traditions of France, "Catholics, like any citizen, have full freedom to prefer one form of government to another, precisely because none of these social forms is in itself opposed to the data of sound reason, nor to the maxims of Christian doctrine."[1]

We can therefore repeat today what Bishop Freppel wrote on the eve of the centenary of the French Revolution:

"In the political sphere, after so many adventures and expedients, each more sterile than the last, we must return frankly and without hesitation to the national monarchy, embodied and personified in the House of France, whose titles and rights derive from a prolonged consent passed down from generation to generation for eight centuries, and not from a mere fleeting vote, wrested by the force of circumstances or seized during a moment of turmoil. We must return to the national monarchy, capable of transformations in the future, as it has been in the past, having successively become feudal, absolute, temperate, and constitutional; to the national monarchy, more capable than any other regime, by the very fixity of its principle, of granting the country and guaranteeing all desirable liberties. No, one can no longer change the temperament of a people any more than that of an individual. No, it is not possible to tear an essential organ from the body of a nation without striking it mortally.

"To maintain a society in the normal conditions of its strength and life, it is necessary above all to preserve in its midst, high and respected, the central institution with which and through which a people was born, lived, grew, developed, becoming one with it, and finding in this fruitful alliance, through the vicissitudes of its history, the sovereign and permanent guarantee of its greatness and unity.

THEORICAL CONCLUSIONS

"To try to reorganize a stable, regular regime, apart from this indispensable factor of political order, would be to fret in a void."[2]

This illuminating page has remained true.

"Christian France can only be saved by a Christian monarchy."[3] But the monarchy must be Christian. A constitutional monarchy, not as Bishop Freppel understood it, but one that acknowledged the sovereignty of the people and left legislative power to their representatives, would not be a Christian monarchy; it would still be the Revolution.

Between the Italian monarchy and the French republic, there is only a nominal difference. It is the same political doctrine, the same principles of government. Between the monarchy of Louis XVI in 1788 and the monarchy of Louis XVI in 1790, there is a world of difference, an abyss, there is the Revolution. Everything, therefore, lies in the principle that governs the institutions.

But who will restore to France this Christian monarchy? If no one thinks of condemning those who hope, no one can impose hope on those who no longer have it.

Among French Catholics, if there are any who believe in the future of a republic in our country, they are free to work towards gathering and preparing its elements. However, there is one condition they cannot avoid fulfilling: an absolute repudiation of all the errors of modern law. This includes reminding the people that they are not the masters, entrusting the threefold power—legislative, judicial, and executive—to the magistrates charged with governing, as God's representatives, removing from public opinion any means of influencing the conduct of state affairs, proclaiming the Catholic religion as the sole religion of the country and its government, and removing from legislation everything contrary to the rights and freedoms of the Church. These are the only conditions under which a constitutional regime can be accepted. We demand them of the monarchy; we cannot exempt the republic from them. Thus amended, the regime would be purged of the principal vices with which it "fails to withstand scrutiny."

Among Catholics who believe they are Republicans, or among Republicans who believe they are Catholics, are there any willing to accept this program?

I don't know, but it is certain that this program is essential for every man of faith and that he must, according to his political opinions, work to subject the monarchy or the republic of the future to it.

It is therefore possible for Catholics to still be divided over hopes, but it is no longer possible to separate in the face of the present.

These people, and they are still the vast majority, will remain faithful to the age-old traditions of the homeland.

These will tend towards a new horizon, but all will have to recognize that the country cannot retain as the foundation of its political constitution the errors of modern law; that it is necessary to abolish universal suffrage and sovereign legislative chambers; finally, above all, to eradicate the heresy of the sovereignty of the people, which is the revolution itself, that is to say, the sin of France.

Chapter Thirteen

Practical Conclusions

The current republic, with its men and its laws, is the punishment of France.

France, the beloved nation, the eldest daughter of the Church, blessed with God's natural and supernatural gifts, France has sinned.

In the same hour of revolt and madness, she denied Christ, her God, and she killed her father, the Most Christian King.

France is being punished.

Since that day of crime, the nation is not only divided, it is mutilated, decapitated.

"It is as punishment for sin that the wicked come to power with God's permission."

Thus concludes Saint Thomas when he examines the means of remedying tyranny:

"We must stop sinning so that the scourge of tyrants may cease."

"Tollenda est igitur culpa ut cesset tyrannorum plaga."[1]

This is the principle from which we must start to find a remedy for our ills.

Tollenda est culpa!

Modern France has a twofold sin.

It contains an original sin: apostasy and regicide, in a word, the Revolution.

There is in it a present sin: the people's claim to sovereignty, the disregard for any authority that does not originate from them; that is to say, impenitence in the sin of revolution.

God, who loves France, makes her feel the weight of his anger.

"Regnare facit hominen hypocritam propter peccata populi. » (Job, XXXIV, 30).

The Jew and the Freemason, the hypocritical man, rule over us.

We must make the people understand why and how they are being punished, if we want them to convert and for God to forgive them.

Therefore, preach, you who speak of God, preach the magnitude of the crime and the justice of atonement. Do not let the people forget that they are guilty. Heirs to ill-gotten gains, they must know it and render it: to Caesar what is Caesar's, to God what is God's.

To Caesar, that is to say to the one who governs on earth, the people must surrender sovereign power, in the temporal order: the authority to make and impose the law.

The people owe it to God to recognize Him as their judge and to profess, as a nation, the worship that He Himself instituted.

We must preach obedience to God first, and then to all those who command in his name and according to his law.

Catholics must learn to hate the Revolution; it must be shown to them in its true light, with its shames, its infamies and its crimes.

Catholics must learn to despise "modern civilization, progress and liberalism", with which the Church, their mother, "must not and cannot be reconciled or compromise."[2]

They must finally break with the errors and illusions of the century, of which most unconsciously suffer oppression.

They must know how to resist in ways other than words; not only by protesting against ungodly laws, but by violating them.

They must claim the freedoms of the Church, not by placing themselves on the condemned ground of common law, but in the name of the higher rights of truth and justice, in the name of Our Lord Jesus Christ, King of Kings.

They must call parliamentarianism a lie, freedom of worship a delusion, liberalism a plague, and popular sovereignty a heresy.

The day when the Catholic people of France, united around their leaders, know how to think, speak and act in this way, the revolution will be over and the homeland saved.

Then it will be easy to agree on the choice of a leader or a form of government. Those who have led us to victory by such a path will know how to do their duty to the very end.

God will shower Catholic France with his gifts, and, victorious over her enemies, will give us masters after his own heart.

Sedem ducum superborum destruxit Deus, et sedere fecit mites pro eis. (Eccli., X, 17.)

Chapter Fourteen

The Obstacle

Many of our readers will surely find the preceding lines too mystical and will see nothing less practical than such a conclusion for such a work.

You who think like this are an obstacle to salvation.

The obstacle to salvation is Catholics who think only of human means, in a peril where only God can save us.

But human resources are not only powerless to save us, they will hasten our ruin. What means do we have, humanly speaking, to save religion and France?

Those given to us by the Constitution.

And what means does the Constitution give us?

Universal suffrage, only.

That is to say, precisely what perpetuates and entrenches in the heart of France the mortal sin of revolution.

That is to say, the grace of the sovereign people, a grace promised at the price of what humiliations and what baseness! A grace always revocable and constantly redeemed.

How can you condemn the dogma of popular sovereignty if you expect salvation from it?

How will you proclaim the inalienable and divine rights of the Church, if the program of the party you are founding to defend it is an electoral program, intended to rally the majority of men of this time?

O infernal trick of the spirit of lies that corners us in this parade!

Pass, O Catholics, under the yoke of popular votes! There is no other way out! Then the failings are prepared; one studies to win over public opinion, one reduces the troublesome baggage of principles to the bare minimum; one is "liberal" friend of "progress" passionate admirer of "modern civilization".

"What is the people," said Saint John Chrysostom, "something filled with tumult and trouble... Is it more miserable than he who serves it? That worldly people should claim to be so is tolerable, although in truth intolerable; but that those who say they have left the world should suffer such an evil is even more intolerable."[1]

And among those who have left the world, there are some who suffer from this evil of the world and whom the world has not left; there are some who claim to reconcile everything, to unite everything: truth with falsehood, light with darkness, the sovereignty of the people with the rights of God.

The triumph of their doctrines is already being celebrated; while remaining enemies of the Church, those who persecute become their friends; souls perish and peace reigns between wolves and shepherds.

We must not awaken the anger of the people, the master will speak, the time of the elections is approaching; silence! By making ourselves very humble, very small, we may perhaps obtain the indulgence we need, to be forgiven for the crime of still existing.

And while we remain silent, error speaks, the thousand voices of the press pour a flood of mud and lies over souls, and we hear nothing but the noise of this flood, and we forget everything, even the language in which truth is spoken; so that if a voice proclaims it, and we hear it, its unknown word produces a scandal or is lost in the night.

Herein lies the obstacle to salvation: it is Catholic liberalism.

Strike the Catholic-Liberals and you will kill the revolution!

NOTES

The Origin of Society and Civil Power

1. De regimine Principum, lib. I, cap. I.

2. Taparelli: Theoretical Essay on Natural Law; Cardinal Zigliara: Philosophia Moralis; Bishop Cavagnis: Notions of Natural and Ecclesiastical Public Law.

3. Genesis: Chapter II, verse 18.

4. Ibid.

5. Genesis: Chapter IV, verse 17.

Nature and Purpose of Civil Society

1. Mgr Cavagnis: Notions de Droit public naturel et ecclésiastique

Civil Power

1. Saint Thomas: De regimine Principum, lib. 1, cap I.

2. Saint Thomas: De regimine Principum, lib. 1, cap I.

3. Epistle of Saint Paul to the Romans chap. XIII, v. 1 and 2): "Let every soul be subject to the higher powers; for there is no power except from God, and those that exist have been ordained by God. Therefore, whoever resists authority resists the ordinance of God." In the encyclical Diuturnum the Pope affirms the doctrine of the Church: "Moreover, as regards political authority, the Church rightly teaches that it proceeds from God; for it finds this clearly attested in Sacred Scripture and in the monuments of Christian antiquity. Nor, moreover, can any doctrine be conceived that is more in harmony either with reason or with the welfare of rulers and peoples alike."

4. Among modern theologians, it suffices to mention Taparelli, Liberatore, Cardinal Zigliara, Bishop Cavagnis, and Father Ferretti. They explain and complete the doctrine taught by Suarez, Bellarmine, and all the Scholastics.

5. Ibid., chap. II.

6. Ibid.

7. De legibus, lib. III, cap. III.

8. Ibid

9. Ibid.

10. De Legibus lib. III, cap. III.

11. Ibid.

12. Ibid.

13. De legibus, lib. 111, cap. IV. 22

14. Ibid.

15. De legibus, lib. III, cap. IV.

16. We will see later how Suarez understands this acceptance.

17. De legibut, lib.III, cap. IV.

18. Ibid.

19. "Quocirca, translatio hujus potestatis a republica in principlem, non est delegatio sed alienatio seu perfecta largitio totius potestatis quae erat in communitate. » De legibus lib. III, cap. IV.

The Best Form of Government

1. De regimine Principum; "Qui perfectam communicantem regit, civitatem vel provinciam, autonomastice rex vocatur." De regimine Princip. Lib. I, cap. I.

2. De Regimine principum, lib. 1, cap. II.

3. Ibid.

4. Ibid.

5. De legibus, lib. III, cap. IV

6. De Regimine principum, lib. I, cap. IV.

7. 5 De Regimine principum, lib. I, cap. V.

8. De Reginime principum, lib. 1, chap. v. A noteworthy fact, which further demonstrates the thought of Saint Thomas, is that, throughout the rest of his book, he speaks only of how a king should govern his kingdom, and that his treatise is dedicated to the king of Cyprus. It should not be inferred from the first of the four propositions cited here that Saint Thomas only admits elective monarchy.

9. De Regimine principum lib. I, cap. VI.

10. These latter are the leaders of a thousand, a hundred and ten men.

11. Jus naturae, lib. II, cap. II, art. 8.

Sovereignty of Man

1. Declaration of the Rights of Man and of the Citizen.

2. Ibid.

3. Encyclical *Immortale Dei*.

Revolutionary Form of Government

1. Jus naturae, lib. II, cap. II, art. 9.

2. There may also be no president, but several consuls or directors; this does not change in any way the essential conditions of the regime.

Judgement of Theologians

1. Jus naturae, part. II, cap. III, art. 4.

2. Jus naturae, lib. II, cap. II, art. 9.

3. Ibid.

4. Liberatore, ut supra.

5. Jus naturae, lib. II, cap. II, art. 9.

6. Jus naturae part. II, cap. III, art. 4, n° 67.

7. Mgr Freppel. La Révolution française, IV.

Doctrines of the Holy See

1. Encyclique Immortale Dei.

2. Ibid.

3. Encyclical Immortale Dei.

4. Ibid.

5. P. V. Maumus. La République et la République de l'Eglise, p. 3

6. Ibid

Theorical Conclusions

1. Encyclique aux évêques et aux catholiques de France.

2. Mgr Freppel La Révolution française, Conclusions.

3. Paroles de M. le comte de Paris.

Practical Conclusions

1. De regemine Principum, lib. 1, cap. IV.

2. Voir la proposition 80, du Syllabus

The Obstacle

1. Saint Jean Chrysostome, In Joann., hom. 3, t. I, p. 8.

www.ingramcontent.com/pod-product-compliance
Lightning Source LLC
Chambersburg PA
CBHW020548030426
42337CB00013B/1015